Discovering
Cultures

Israel

Jennifer Rozines Roy

***B*ENCHMARK *B*OOKS**

MARSHALL CAVENDISH
NEW YORK

Benchmark Books
Marshall Cavendish
99 White Plains Road
Tarrytown, New York 10591-9001
www.marshallcavendish.com

Library of Congress Cataloging-in-Publication Data

Roy, Jennifer Rozines, 1967–
Israel / by Jennifer Rozines Roy.
p. cm. — (Discovering cultures)
Includes bibliographical references and index.
Summary: Highlights the geography, people, food, schools, recreation, celebrations, and language of Israel.
ISBN 0-7614-1720-6
1. Israel—Juvenile literature. [1. Israel.] I. Title. II. Series.
DS118.R69 2003
956.94—dc21   2003008127

Photo Research by Candlepants Incorporated
Cover Photo: *Corbis*/Richard T. Nowitz

The photographs in this book are used by permission and through the courtesy of; *Richard T. Nowitz*: 1, 22, 35, 37, 38. *Corbis*: Richard T. Nowitz, 4, 12, 14 (left and right), 25 (top), 29, 31, 34, 43 (top left); James Marshall, 6; Koren Ziv, 7 (top), 42 (top right); Hanan Isacher, 7 (lower); Shai Ginott, 8, 43 (lower left); Carl & Ann Purcell, 9, 43 (middle right); Dave G. Houser, 10, 21; Annie Griffiths Belt, 11, 20, 28, 30, 42 (lower right); Morton Beebe, 13; Paul A. Souders, 15, 17 (top); David H. Wells, 16, 25 (lower); Ricki Rosen, 17 (lower), 24; Buddy Mays 18-19; Nik Wheeler, 26; Robert Holmes, 32; Dave Bartruff, 36, back cover; David Rubinger, 44 (top); Pimentel Jean/KIPA, 44 (lower); AFP, 45.

Cover: *The Western Wall at dusk*; Title page: *Young girl celebrates Israeli Independence Day*

Map and illustrations by Ian Warpole
Book design by Virginia Pope

Printed in China
1 3 5 6 4 2

Turn the Pages...

Where in the World Is Israel?

Israel is a country in the Middle East. It lies in Asia and forms a bridge between the continents of Asia, Europe, and Africa. Long and narrow, Israel sits on the eastern shore of the Mediterranean Sea. Its neighbors are Lebanon, Syria, Jordan, and Egypt.

Israel is small. It is about the size of the state of New Jersey. You can drive a car across its widest part in less than two hours! From the north to the south, it takes only seven hours.

Poppies bloom in the hills of Galilee.

Map of Israel

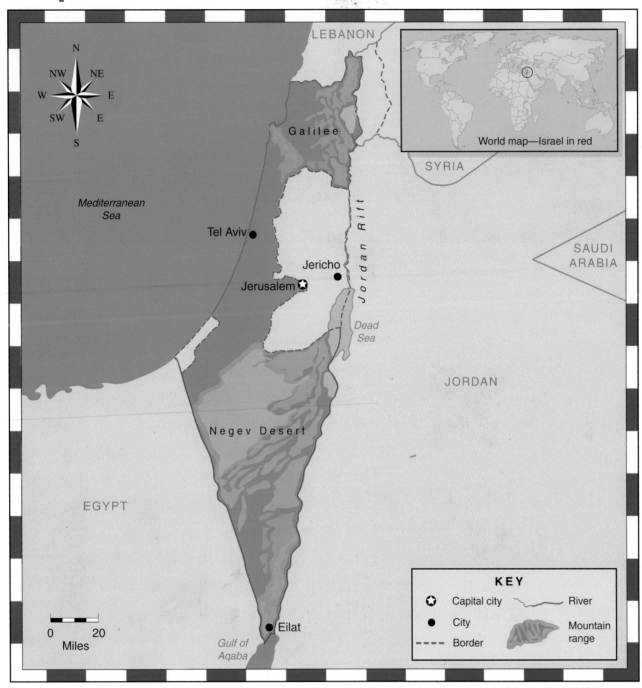

LEBANON

N
NW NE
W   E
SW SE
S

Galilee

Mediterranean
Sea

SYRIA

World map—Israel in red

SAUDI
ARABIA

Tel Aviv ●

Jericho ●
Jerusalem ✪

Jordan Rift

Dead
Sea

JORDAN

Negev Desert

EGYPT

● Eilat

0   20
Miles

Gulf of
Aqaba

KEY

✪ Capital city   River

● City   Mountain
                       range
- - - Border

Skyline of Tel Aviv

Israel has two seasons—winter and summer. Winters are mild and rainy. Summers are long, hot, and dry. Israel's weather is different from place to place. You can go skiing down a snowy mountain and swim at a sunny seashore all on the same day!

Israel also has many different landforms. More than half of Israelis live along the coast on the Mediterranean Sea. This area is known as the coastal plain. The modern, busy city of Tel Aviv sits right on the sea. Thousands of people visit its white, sandy beaches. The rich soil of the coastal plain is important for farming. Juicy oranges, lemons, grapefruits, avocados, and strawberries are grown there.

Another area well known for its crops lies in northern Israel. In the hills of Galilee, farmers grow olives, figs, and grapes. They also raise poultry and cattle. This area is colder and rainier than the rest of the country. It has snow-topped mountains and green valleys.

The capital city of Jerusalem sits in the center of Israel. Jerusalem is Israel's largest city. It is considered holy by three of the world's major religions—Judaism,

Jerusalem's buildings are both old and new.

The Dead Sea is the lowest water surface on earth.

Islam, and Christianity. Jerusalem is a blend of the old and new. There are many monuments that are thousands of years old. There are also museums, government buildings, and shopping malls. Many of the buildings in Jerusalem are made from golden-yellow stone. Their golden color makes the city seem to glow in the evening.

The Jordan Rift is a deep valley. This hot, humid region includes the lowest water surface on earth—the Dead Sea. One of the world's oldest cities, Jericho, is also in the valley.

The Negev Desert forms the southern part of Israel. The Negev is extremely hot and dry, with stony cliffs and giant craters. Dusty

Rocky cliffs rise above the Negev Desert.

sandstorms blow across the land. Very little rain falls in the desert. Only the strongest desert plants and animals can live there.

At the southern tip of Israel lies the city of Eilat. It sits on the Gulf of Aqaba. Vacationers come to its beautiful beaches. They dive under the clear blue waters to see the colorful tropical fish and coral reefs.

Israel is filled with nature reserves. The reserves are protected areas of land and water. Rare plants and wild animals can live safely there.

With its many fascinating places and sights, Israel is truly a unique country!

The Dead Sea

Walk into the Dead Sea and lift up your feet. You will float! You cannot sink in this sea. The water has so much salt and minerals in it that it lifts you up. You can even read a book while floating in it, and the pages will not get wet!

It is called the Dead Sea because no fish and few plants can live in the salt water. The Dead Sea is the lowest water surface on Earth—almost 1,338 feet (408 meters) below sea level.

Many people think that the minerals in the Dead Sea mud are good for the skin. Visitors scoop the thick black mud over their bodies and let it dry out in the sun. Then the "mud people" wash off and go for a float!

What Makes Israel Israeli?

A child sits on the Fountain of the Lion.

What makes Israel Israeli? The blending of the old and the new! People have lived in this part of the Middle East for thousands of years. But the modern nation of Israel is quite new. It was created less than sixty years ago, in 1948.

The common bond between most Israelis is that they are Jewish. Judaism is a way of life in Israel. It affects how the government works, and how schools and businesses are run.

The majority of Israelis —about 80 percent—are

Jews walk by a Muslim woman in Jerusalem.

Jews. They practice a religion called Judaism. The next largest group are Muslim Arabs. Their religion is called Islam. There are also many Christians living in Israel.

People born in Israel are known as *sabras*. Sabra is a cactus fruit that is prickly on the outside but sweet on the inside. Many Israelis describe themselves that way. They may act tough or seem bold, but are also very caring and joyous.

Many Israelis were not born in Israel. Like the United States, Israel is a melting pot of different cultures. It is a country of many immigrants. Millions of Jews have come from other countries to make Israel their home. They have come from the former Soviet Union (now the Russian Federation), Africa, Europe, and America. They have brought with them their own customs and beliefs.

Israel is a democracy. Its people are free to worship and live any way they want. So there are many different ways of life, depending on where people come from and the community in which they live.

The official languages of Israel are Hebrew and Arabic. Both are very old languages. Some English words borrowed from Hebrew are lemon (*limon*), sack

Russian musicians perform on a street corner.

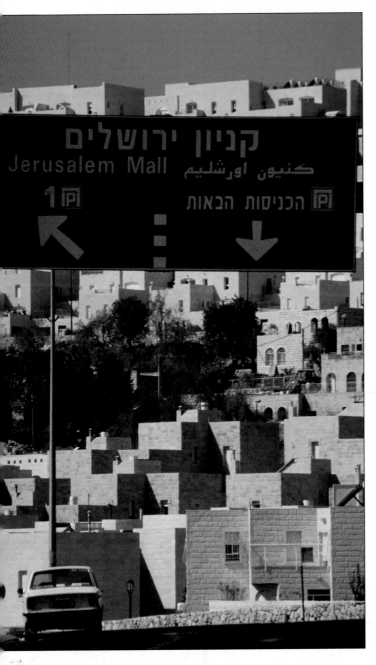
This way to the Jerusalem shopping mall

(*sok*), and cinnamon (*kimmamon*). The words *zero*, *cotton*, and *almanac* trace their roots from Arabic. Israelis have had to add many newer words to keep up with modern times. Speakers from ancient days did not use a *makshev* (computer), ride *amatos* (airplanes), or talk on a *tiliphon* (telephone)!

Most Israelis speak English. In fact, road signs on highways often give directions in Hebrew, Arabic, and English. Some Israelis may also speak French, Russian, Polish, or German. It is not uncommon to hear people in shops or restaurants speaking many different languages.

Music, dance, and art are important to the Israeli people. Israelis love music. They enjoy listening to classical, jazz, or pop music in the theater, on the radio, or on MTV. Israel also has its own folk music. These songs express thoughts about peace and war, hope and sadness, and life in Israel.

Dance is a big part of Israeli life. Adults and children enjoy folk dances

Young dancers perform a ballet.

A potter at work

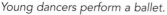

like the *hora*, an eastern European circle dance. Modern dance, ballet, and disco are also popular.

Israel is known for its fine arts and crafts. Gold and silver jewelry, stone sculptures, paintings, and pottery are made by hand. Artists also make wine cups, candlesticks, and festive plates. These works of art are used in Jewish homes all over the world. Arab Israelis create crafts from wood, leather, and blown glass.

So what makes Israel Israeli? Creativity, hard work, and hope. Israelis hope that the nation they have worked so hard to build will grow stronger and safer. They want it to remain a special place in the world.

Traditional Dress

Walk around a city in Israel, and you will see people wearing the same kinds of clothing that Americans wear. Israelis wear jeans, t-shirts with American logos, and all the latest fashions. Since it is often warm, you will notice people in sandals and sunglasses all year round. Many Israeli boys and men add something else to their outfit— a *kipa*. A kipa is a round cloth or knitted cap that is worn by religious Jewish males.

Very religious Jews, called *Hasidim*, wear more traditional clothes. Hasidic men wear black suits and white shirts. They grow beards. Boys wear white shirts and black pants. On either side of the boys' heads are two curls of long hair. Hasidic women and girls wear long skirts and long-sleeved shirts. When a girl marries, she must cut her hair short and wear a wig or head covering.

Living in Israel

Most Israelis live in a city or just outside of one. They live in modern apartments in tall buildings or in private houses. Because there is not much space in Israel, homes are not very large. Inside they look like American homes, with TVs, VCRs, computers, and microwaves. Children have toys, games, and books. Teenagers decorate their walls with posters of music groups and sports stars. Outside, the neighborhood can be bustling with cars, buses, and people.

Some Israelis choose to live on a *kibbutz*. They are called kibbutzniks. A kibbutz is a community where all the members are expected to work together like one large family. Kibbutz members run farms and businesses and share everything that is earned. No money is needed—the

An Israeli family surfs the Internet.

A kibbutznik picks ripe cantaloupes.

Children at play on a kibbutz

kibbutz provides food, clothing, and transportation to all its members. Kibbutzniks often eat together in a large dining hall and attend planned social events.

For many years, children on a kibbutz were raised in separate houses with boys and girls of their own age group. They played, went to

school, and did chores during the day. In the evening, they visited their parents' living quarters. Then they returned to the children's houses to sleep. These days, kibbutz children live with their parents. They still spend plenty of time with the other kibbutz kids. This makes them feel like they grow up with many brothers and sisters.

A group of Israeli people called the *bedouin* lives in the Negev Desert. Bedouins live in black goatskin tents and wander from place to place with their families. The bedouin herd sheep and goats and travel on camels. In recent years, many bedouin have given up their wandering and settled in desert communities.

A bedouin boy leads his donkeys acros the desert.

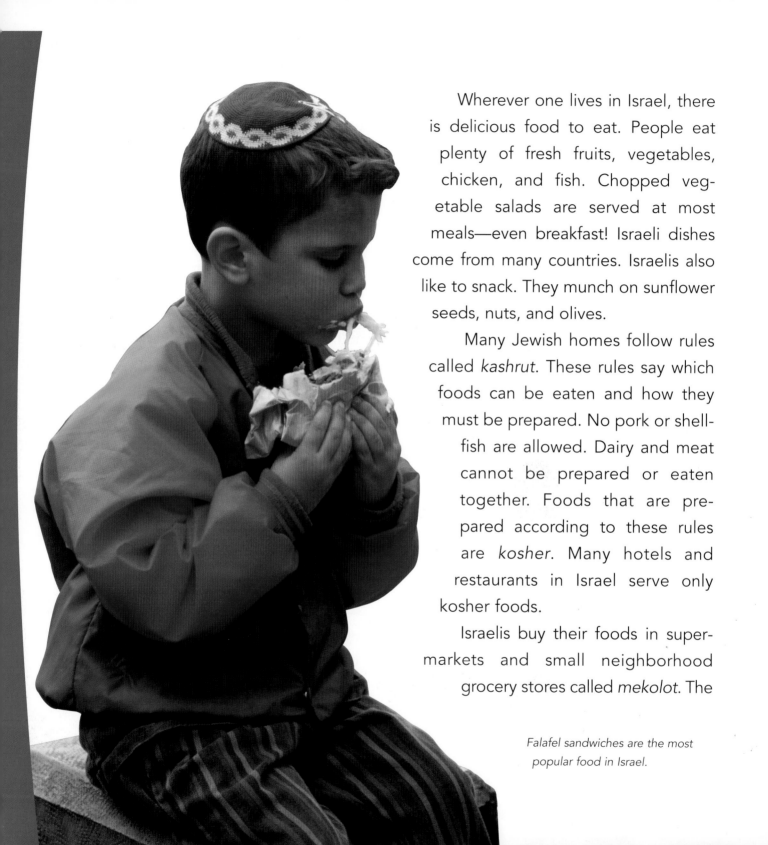

Wherever one lives in Israel, there is delicious food to eat. People eat plenty of fresh fruits, vegetables, chicken, and fish. Chopped vegetable salads are served at most meals—even breakfast! Israeli dishes come from many countries. Israelis also like to snack. They munch on sunflower seeds, nuts, and olives.

Many Jewish homes follow rules called *kashrut*. These rules say which foods can be eaten and how they must be prepared. No pork or shellfish are allowed. Dairy and meat cannot be prepared or eaten together. Foods that are prepared according to these rules are *kosher*. Many hotels and restaurants in Israel serve only kosher foods.

Israelis buy their foods in supermarkets and small neighborhood grocery stores called *mekolot*. The

Falafel sandwiches are the most popular food in Israel.

outdoor markets are popular, too. There, customers can get good bargains on fresh foods. Israelis also love fast food. They go for hamburgers and Cokes at McDonald's and eat pizza at Pizza Hut.

On Friday evenings, families come together to light candles, give blessings, and eat a special meal. The Jewish day of rest, the *Sabbath*, begins at sunset on

Fresh fruits and vegetables in the market

A Shabbat table

Friday and lasts through sunset on Saturday. Most of Israel observes the Sabbath. Stores, offices, and public transportation close down during this time. The Israeli people, who work hard six days a week, enjoy spending the Sabbath with family and friends. As they say in Israel, "Shabbat Shalom (Good Sabbath)!"

Let's Eat!
Falafel

What is the most popular fast food in Israel? Falafel! Falafel is stuffed into flat pita bread pockets and topped with onions and cucumbers. It is sold at street stands in every city and town around Israel. Ask an adult to help you prepare this recipe.

Ingredients:

1 pound canned chickpeas, drained

1 cup bread crumbs

1 tablespoon chopped parsley

1 egg

1 teaspoon salt

1 teaspoon garlic powder

1 teaspoon dried hot red peppers

vegetable oil

Wash your hands. Mash the chickpeas in a bowl. Add the garlic powder, salt, peppers, and bread crumbs, and mix. Add the egg and mix again. Shape the mixture into small balls about 1 inch (2.5 centimeters) around. Heat the oil in a frying pan on the stove. Gently drop a few of the balls into the pan. Turn them until they are golden brown on the outside. Use a spoon to take them out. Place them on a plate covered with paper towels. Serves four people.

School Days

Israelis believe that education is very important. All children from the ages of five to sixteen must attend school. They go to primary school for six years, junior high for three years, and high school for three years. Israeli families can choose from different types of schools. Some schools are general schools. These are not religious. Others are religious schools. There are separate schools for Jewish, Arab, and Christian children.

Students go to school six days a week. Friday is a half day. There is no school on Saturdays. The children study math, science, social studies, music, computers, and crafts. They learn to read, speak, and write Hebrew and English. In religious schools, Jewish children also study the Bible. Arab students learn Arabic. They take classes about Islam and about Arab history.

Israeli high school students may take classes in farming, electronics, and

Israeli schoolchildren study religion in the classroom.

Studying eels for a science project

Young students paint pictures for art class.

military studies. After they graduate from high school, almost every young man and woman joins the Israeli army. Israeli children grow up knowing that when they are eighteen years old they will enter the military. Young men stay in the army for at least three years. Young women are in for twenty-one months. After the army, many go to college.

The *ulpan* is a special school for all children and grown-ups who have moved to Israel. The ulpan is very helpful to these newcomers. They learn about Israeli culture and how to speak Hebrew.

After school, when students are not doing homework, they may play sports. Some go to a school club or youth group. Other children go straight home from school. They make their own snack, finish their homework, and watch television while their parents are still at work. Children who come home alone after school are called *yeled mesteach*. These children learn to be responsible at a young age.

Israeli children are expected to clean up after themselves and not get into trouble. When their parents come home, children are asked all about their school day. Israeli parents are very interested in what their children are learning. Like parents in the United States, they are very proud when their children get good grades!

Most Israeli children enjoy using computers.

Learning Hebrew

Israeli schoolchildren learn to read Hebrew beginning in kinder-garten, just like American students learn English. But there are differences between the two languages. The Hebrew alphabet looks and sounds different than English. And Hebrew is written right to left! So you open a Hebrew book from the back, which is really the front for Israelis. Then you start to read from the right side of the page and follow the words to the left. Hebrew has no capital letters and is printed without vowels, except in books for very young children.

Here is the Hebrew alphabet:

א	aleph	ל	lamed
ב	bet	מ	mem
ג	gimel	נ	nun
ד	dalet	ס	samech
ה	heh	ע	ayin
ו	vav	פ	peh
ז	zayin	צ	tzadi
ח	het	ק	kuf
ט	tet	ר	resh
י	youd	ש	shin
כ	kaf	ת	taf

Just for Fun

What do Israeli children do in their free time? They have fun! Children in Israel do many of the same things as children in the United States. They enjoy playing handheld video games, surfing the Internet, going to the movies, and hanging out with friends. Israelis read a lot in their free time, too. Children enjoy reading comic

It is fun to spend time with friends at the beach!

books. Israel even has its own comic superhero called Sabraman.

Israelis are very active and enjoy being outdoors. They go hiking, jogging, and camping. They often visit the seashore and play volleyball and *matkot*, a paddleball game on the beach. Sports are very important to Israelis. Soccer and basketball are the most popular sports. Many kids play in youth leagues and dream of some day making the Israeli professional teams.

Besides sports teams, Israeli children participate in youth groups. They wear khaki uniforms and learn outdoor skills and games. They also volunteer on farms and in hospitals.

An Israeli boy builds a sand castle.

Israeli boy scouts sit on the grass.

Another outdoor activity Israelis enjoy is archaeology. Adults and children dig in the earth for hidden treasures from the past. They find pottery, coins, weapons, and writings. These things help people learn what life in Israel was like thousands of years ago.

Israeli kids like to watch television. Little children love *Rehov Sum-Sum*, which is Hebrew *Sesame Street*. The characters on this show are not exactly like the American ones. Instead of Big Bird, there is a kind of porcupine named Kippie. And Cookie Monster is Oogie, because the Hebrew word for cookie is *oogiyah*. Older children watch American shows like *Friends* and *Dawson's Creek*. They also see music television from two different continents—MTV Europe and MTV Asia. And everybody enjoys cartoons.

An archaeologist shows children ancient pieces of pottery.

Israelis watch the news a lot. Even the children keep up with what is happening in their country and around the world. Since the time Israel became a nation, it has been fighting with its Arab neighbors. They have fought three wars. Arabs believe that Israel should belong to them and not to the Jewish people. The constant fighting has upset both the Jews and Arabs.

There have been many tries at peace, but the Middle East is still very troubled. Israeli children are forced to be aware of the dangers in their country.

Sometimes they want to go somewhere or attend an event. But their parents say "no" because they are afraid that terrorists might attack. The Israeli army tries hard to protect all its citizens. Everywhere you go in Israel, from soccer games to beaches to shopping centers, you will see soldiers.

Despite the serious side of living in Israel, children really do have loads of fun. They are hopeful that peace will come. They laugh and play just like kids everywhere.

Israeli children riding the school bus

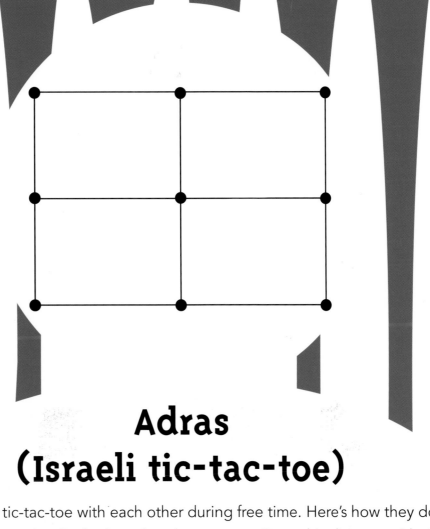

Adras
(Israeli tic-tac-toe)

Children play tic-tac-toe with each other during free time. Here's how they do it. Two children can play. Each player has three stones. Draw this diagram with chalk on a sidewalk or scratch it into the sand. Take turns placing a stone on one of the intersections (points where the lines meet). The winner is the first player to get three of his or her stones in a line up, down, sideways, or diagonally.

Let's Celebrate!

Israelis celebrate many holidays. Most of their holidays come from stories about Jewish people. Some are serious and some are fun. Israeli holidays fall on different days every year. Israelis check the Jewish calendar to make sure they do not miss any of their festivals!

The Jewish New Year, Rosh Hashanah, is observed in autumn. Jews celebrate the new year by blowing a ram's horn called a shofar. They eat foods dipped in honey and hope for a "sweet" new year. Ten days later comes Yom Kippur, a serious holy day. On this day, religious Jews do not eat or drink. They ask God to forgive them for anything they have done wrong. On Yom Kippur, all of Israel

A rabbi blows the ram's horn.

seems to be silent. Few cars are on the street. Airplanes do not fly, and there are no Israeli radio or television broadcasts. The holiday ends with a large meal shared by hungry families.

Another Jewish festival is Hanukkah. Hanukkah is usually in December and lasts eight days. It celebrates a victory in a war that was fought over 2,000 years ago. Hanukkah is the festival of lights. For eight nights, Jews light candles in a candleholder called a *menorah.* They sing blessings, eat potato latkes (pancakes), and play a game with a spinning top called a dreidl.

In early spring, children dress up in costumes and celebrate Purim. Purim

Lighting the menorah

35

Wearing costumes for Purim

is a little like Halloween. But instead of trick-or-treating, Israeli children celebrate by giving gifts to friends, family, and the poor. They also go to cheerful religious services, where everyone dances and sings.

Every spring, Jewish people celebrate a festival that is more than 3,000 years old. It is called Pesach, or Passover. Families gather for the *seder* dinner. They eat special foods that help tell the story of the Jews' escape from slavery in Egypt. During the eight days of Passover, Jews eat crispy, flat bread called matzah. During the Passover seder, a piece of matzah is hidden in the house. All the children hunt for it. The lucky child who finds it wins money.

Each year in May, the people of Israel celebrate their own country. On Memorial Day, they remember the people who died fighting for Israel. At sundown, the sadness turns into joy as Independence Day begins. There are

A Jewish family gathers for the seder.

carnivals, parades, airplane shows, and fireworks to celebrate the day Israel became a nation.

Israeli Arabs also celebrate holidays. The most joyful is the three-day feast called Id-al-Fitr. Id-al-Fitr takes place at the end of Ramadan. Ramadan is the ninth month of the Muslim year, considered a holy month in Islam. It usually comes in

Fireworks over the walls of Jerusalem's Old City

November or December each year. On Id-al-Fitr, families visit each other and children receive presents. People dye their hands with a red-orange dye called henna for good luck.

Israelis like to sing and dance and celebrate life. Their holidays bring families, communities, and the country together.

Dance the Hora

A common way to celebrate an Israeli festival is by doing the national dance, the hora. The hora is a folk dance with six steps that you do over and over.

1. Step right with your right foot

2. Cross your left foot behind your right foot

3. Step right with your right foot

4. Hop on your right foot

5. Step left with your left foot

6. Hop on your left foot

Practice these steps, then join some friends. Form a circle and hold hands—or even trickier, put your hands on each other's shoulders, and dance the hora to some festive music. Build up speed, and you will be whirling and twirling around!

The colors of the Israeli flag are blue and white. The six-pointed star in the center is the Star of David, a symbol of Judaism.

Israelis use shekels for money. The silver shekel is about the size of an American dime, but thicker. The exchange rate often changes, but in 2003 about 4.5 shekels equaled one U.S. dollar.

Count in Hebrew

English	Hebrew	Say it like this:
one	echad	ah-HAHT
two	shtayim	shtah-YEEM
three	shalosh	shah-LOSH
four	arba	ar-BAH
five	chamesh	hah-MAYSH
six	shesh	shesh
seven	sheva	SHEH-vah
eight	shmoneh	SHMOH-neh
nine	teisha	TAY-shah
ten	esser	EH-sair

Glossary

bedouin   (BEH-duh-wuhn) Group of traveling people.

falafel   Fried balls of spicy ground chickpeas.

Hasidim   Group of people who follow strict religious Jewish laws.

kibbutz   Communal settlement where people work and live together.

kosher   (KOH-shur) Food that has been prepared according to Jewish law.

menorah   Candleholder with nine branches that is used in Jewish ceremonies.

Sabbath   Seventh day of the week (Saturday); the day of rest for Jews.

sabra   Nickname for a person born in Israel; comes from the name of a cactus fruit.

seder (SAY-dur)   A special Passover dinner that recalls the Jews' escape from Egypt.

ulpan (ool-PAHN)   School that teaches immigrants how to speak Hebrew.

Fast Facts

Galilee

Tel Aviv

Jericho

Jerusalem

Negev Desert

Eilat

Israel is small. It is about the size of the state of New Jersey.

The capital city of Jerusalem sits in the center of Israel. Jerusalem is Israel's largest city.

The modern nation of Israel was created less than sixty years ago, in 1948.

Israelis use shekels for money.

The colors of the Israeli flag are blue and white. The six-pointed star in the center is the Star of David.

As of July 2002, there were 6,029,529 people living in Israel.

In 2003, 80.1 percent of the Israeli people were Jewish, 14.6 percent were Muslim, 2.1 percent were Christian, and 3.2 percent followed other religions.

Israel has two seasons—winter and summer. Winters are mild and rainy. Summers are long, hot, and dry.

The Dead Sea is the lowest water surface on Earth—almost 1,338 feet (408 m) below sea level.

The official languages of Israel are Hebrew and Arabic.

Israel is a democracy. Its people are free to live any way they want.

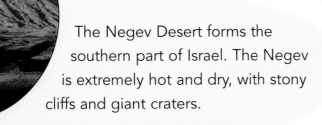

The Negev Desert forms the southern part of Israel. The Negev is extremely hot and dry, with stony cliffs and giant craters.

Proud to Be Israeli

Golda Meir (1898–1978)

Golda Meir was one of Israel's founders and greatest heroines. She was born Goldie Mabovitz in Kiev, Ukraine. As a child, she saw violence against her fellow Jews. Mabovitz's family moved to the United States to escape the danger.

When Mabovitz grew up, she decided to help build a Jewish homeland where her people could be safe. In 1921, she emigrated to the land of Israel (then called Palestine). Mabovitz changed her name to a Hebrew name, Golda Meir, and joined a kibbutz. She became active in politics. She signed the independence proclamation that officially made Israel a country.

Golda Meir became the first female prime minister of Israel in 1969. She led the country through difficult times and resigned in 1974. When she died four years later, people around the world mourned for this great lady.

Itzhak Perlman (1945–   )

One of the most famous violinists in the world comes from Israel. His name is Itzhak Perlman. Born in Tel Aviv, he became ill with polio as a child. Although the disease weakened his muscles, he went on to become an expert violinist. When he was thirteen, he moved to the United States to join a traveling music group. When he was nineteen, he won a major competition. That made him famous. Since then, he has played the violin all over the world with many orchestras and performers. He joined the Israel Philharmonic Orchestra in history-making concerts in the Soviet Union. Itzhak Perlman has won many Grammy awards for his albums and recorded music for movies. He also teaches young musicians and speaks about living a full life despite his disability.

Colonel Ilan Ramon (1955–2003)

Colonel Ilan Ramon made history as the first Israeli in space. In January 2003, Colonel Ramon joined six U.S. astronauts on the space shuttle Columbia. The space shuttle orbited Earth for over two weeks. Tragically, the shuttle broke apart as it was coming in for a landing. All of the astronauts on board were killed as the shuttle exploded.

While in space, Colonel Ramon worked on an experiment known as MEIDEX, the Mediterranean Israeli Dust Experiment. The MEIDEX project studies dust particles to see how these particles affect weather in the Middle East.

Ilan Ramon was born in 1955 in Israel. He went to high school in Tel Aviv and then entered the Israeli air force to train to be a pilot. Then he earned a college degree in electronics and computer engineering. Ramon next flew aircraft and headed flight operations in the air force and moved up the ranks to become a Colonel. Ramon was selected to train at NASA (National Aeronautics and Space Administration). So he, his wife, and four children moved to Houston, Texas, where he trained to become an astronaut.

Colonel Ramon felt that he represented all the Israeli people. When he died, the whole country of Israel mourned.

Find Out More

Books

Festivals of the World: Israel by Don Foy. Gareth Stevens Publishing, Milwaukee, WI, 1997.

Food and Festivals: Israel by Ronne Randall. Steck-Vaughn, Austin, TX, 1999.

Children of Israel by Laurie M. Grossman. Carolrhoda Books, Minneapolis, MN, 2000.

Nations of the World: Israel by Jen Green. Raintree Steck-Vaughn, Austin, TX, 2001.

Web Sites

For more information about Israel visit the Israeli Government's Tourist Office Web site at **www.infotour.co.il**.

Go to **www.yahooligans.com/around_the_world/countries/Israel/** for pictures and maps of Israel.

Video

Touring Israel: The Nation for the Next Millenium (1999), Questar Inc.

Index

Page numbers for illustrations are in **boldface.**

About the Author

Jennifer Rozines Roy is the author of more than twenty books for young people. A former Gifted and Talented teacher, she holds a B.S. in psychology and an M.A. in elementary education. Ms. Roy has visited Israel and thinks it is one of the most amazing places in the world. She lives in upstate New York with her husband Gregory and son Adam.

Acknowledgments

My thanks to Amy and Robin Rozines, Julia DeVillers, Mina Halperin, Haya Nissim, the Urmans, and Greg Roy.